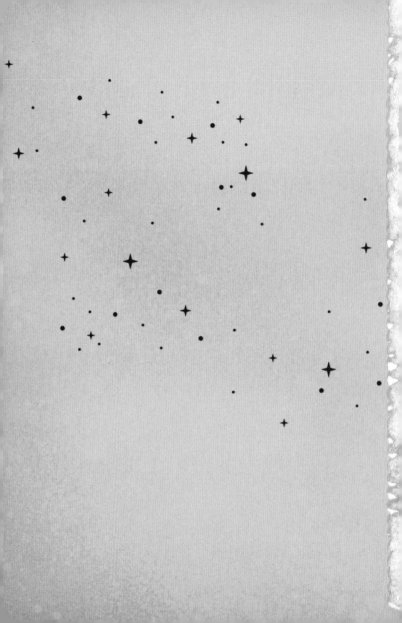

TO

_____

FROM

_____

DATE

_____

PROMISES

FROM GOD'S HEART

COMFORTING TRUTH
FOR YOUR EVERY NEED

LIVE YOUR FAITH

Promises from God's Heart: Comforting Truth for Your Every Need
Copyright © 2022 by DaySpring
First Edition, January 2022

Published by:

21154 Highway 16 East
Siloam Springs, AR 72761
dayspring.com

Compiled by Lisa Stilwell
Cover Design by Hannah Skelton
Typeset by Becca Barnett

Printed in China
Prime: J7098
ISBN: 978-1-64870-324-9

CONTENTS

INTRODUCTION

"I PROMISE!"

These two words are so simple, yet they are filled with power and anticipation of something binding and strong. We hear and say them from the time we first form words. Parents promise to be there for us, friends promise to be our best friend forever, and as we get older, fiancés promises to be ours "till death do us part." But as we grow, it doesn't take long to realize that not everyone keeps his or her promises—and with every broken promise falls a broken piece of heart. When that happens, how do we know who to believe and trust anymore?

Well, there is One who can always be trusted—He's got a perfect record for keeping promises. God and His Word are full of assurances that have remained true and reliable since the beginning of time. Just as He promised prophets and disciples from the Old and New Testaments, He hears your every prayer today and vows to give you hope that you can believe in. If you are trying to overcome fear, He promises to give you His courage. If you are hurting, He will give comfort and fill you with peace. There are hundreds of them filled with His commitment of love and faithfulness, provision and grace, and so much more.

No matter where you are in life or what circumstance in which you find yourself, He's made pledges straight from His heart to yours to help you through each day and every need of your journey. Read them, memorize them, and know with full confidence that you are loved and cared for with the greatest capacity ever known to humankind. Those are just a few of God's promises to you.

For all God's words are right,
and everything He does is
worthy of our trust.

PSALM 33:4 *TLB*

JUST THINK,
  You're here not by chance,
  but by God's choosing.
  His hand formed you
  and made you the person you are.
  He compares you to no one else—
  you are one of a kind.
  You lack nothing
  that His grace can't give you.
  He has allowed you to be here
  at this time in history
  to fulfill His special purpose
  for this generation.
  —*Roy Lessin*

To every thing there is a season,
  and a time to every purpose
    under the heaven.

Ecclesiastes 3:1 KJV

PROMISES *from* GOD'S HEART
FOR *acceptance…*

The LORD said to Samuel, "Don't judge by his appearance or height, for I have rejected him. The LORD doesn't see things the way you see them. People judge by outward appearance, but the LORD looks at the heart."

1 Samuel 16:7 NLT

Those who welcome you are welcoming Me. And when they welcome Me they are welcoming God who sent me.

Matthew 10:40 TLB

*Accept one another, then,
just as Christ accepted you, in
order to bring praise to God.*

ROMANS 15:7 NIV

If the readiness is there, it is acceptable according to what a person has, not according to what he does not have.

II CORINTHIANS 8:12 ESV

We are no longer Jews or Greeks
or slaves or free men or even
merely men or women, but we
are all the same—we are Christians;
we are one in Christ Jesus.

Galatians 3:28 TLB

Love others as well as you love yourself.

Mark 12:31 THE MESSAGE

*If possible, so far as it depends on
you, live peaceably with all.*

ROMANS 12:18 ESV

PROMISES *from* GOD'S HEART
WHEN YOU ARE *afraid*...

God is our refuge and strength,
a helper who is always found in times of
trouble. Therefore we will not be afraid.

Psalm 46:1–2 CSB

The LORD is my light and my salvation—
whom shall I fear? The LORD is the stronghold of my life—of whom shall I be afraid?

Psalm 27:1 NIV

There is no fear in love;
instead, perfect love drives
out fear, because fear involves
punishment. So the
one who fears is not
complete in love.

1 JOHN 4:18 CSB

*You did not receive the spirit
of slavery to fall back into fear,
but you have received the
Spirit of adoption as sons, by
whom we cry, "Abba! Father!"*

ROMANS 8:15 ESV

Fear not, for I am with you;
be not dismayed, for I am your God;
I will strengthen you, I will help
you, I will uphold you with my
righteous right hand.

Isaiah 41:10 ESV

In my distress I called to the LORD;
I called out to my God.
From His temple He heard my voice;
my cry came to His ears.

2 Samuel 22:7 NIV

We have this hope as an anchor
for the soul, firm and secure.

Hebrews 6:19 CSB

You have been a stronghold
for the poor person, a stronghold for the
needy in his distress, a refuge from
storms and a shade from heat.

Isaiah 25:4 CSB

*Whoever listens to Me will live
securely and be undisturbed by
the dread of danger.*

PROVERBS 1:33 CSB

PROMISES *from* GOD'S HEART
WHEN YOU ARE *angry...*

✦ ✢

Don't hit back; discover beauty in everyone.
If you've got it in you, get along with everybody.
Don't insist on getting even; that's not for you
to do. "I'll do the judging," says God.
"I'll take care of it."

Romans 12:19 THE MESSAGE

If you forgive those who sin against you,
your heavenly Father will forgive you.

Matthew 6:14 NLT

*Refrain from anger and give up
your rage; do not be agitated—it
can only bring harm.*

PSALM 37:8 CSB

Stop being mean, bad-tempered, and angry. Quarreling, harsh words, and dislike of others should have no place in your lives. Instead, be kind to each other, tenderhearted, forgiving one another, just as God has forgiven you because you belong to Christ.

EPHESIANS 4:31–32 TLB

A gentle answer turns away anger, but a harsh word stirs up wrath.

Proverbs 15:1 CSB

The LORD is slow to anger and filled with unfailing love, forgiving every kind of sin and rebellion.

Numbers 14:18 NLT

Be completely humble and gentle; be patient, bearing with one another in love. Make every effort to keep the unity of the Spirit through the bond of peace. . . . To each one of us grace has been given as Christ apportioned it.

EPHESIANS 4:2-3 NIV

Sing to the LORD, all you godly ones! Praise His holy name. For His anger lasts only a moment, but His favor lasts a lifetime! Weeping may last through the night, but joy comes with the morning.

Psalm 30:4–5 NLT

PROMISES *from* GOD'S HEART
WHEN YOU ARE *anxious*...

✦ ✦

Don't worry about anything, but in
everything, through prayer and petition
with thanksgiving, present your requests
to God. And the peace of God, which
surpasses all understanding, will guard your
hearts and minds in Christ Jesus.

Philippians 4:6–7 CSB

*Those who know Your
name trust in You, for You,
LORD, have never forsaken
those who seek You.*

PSALM 9:10 NIV

Don't have so little faith! Don't always think about what you will eat or what you will drink. Don't worry about it. All the people in the world are trying to get those things. Your Father knows that you need them.

LUKE 12:28–30 ICB

Remember, your Father
knows exactly what you need
even before you ask Him!

Matthew 6:8 TLB

Trust in the LORD with all your heart;
do not depend on your own understanding.
Seek His will in all you do, and He will show
you which path to take.

Proverbs 3:5–6 NLT

Seek first His kingdom and His righteousness, and all these things will be given to you as well. Therefore do not worry about tomorrow, for tomorrow will worry about itself. Each day has enough trouble of its own.

MATTHEW 6:33–34 NIV

Be still in the presence of the LORD, and wait patiently for Him to act.

Psalm 37:7 NLT

Humble yourselves, therefore, under God's mighty hand, that He may lift you up in due time. Cast all your anxiety on Him because He cares for you.

1 Peter 5:6-7 NIV

Cast your burden on the LORD,
and He will sustain you; He will never
allow the righteous to be shaken.

Psalm 55:22 CSB

Peace I leave with you.
My peace I give to you.
I do not give to you as the world
gives. Don't let your heart be
troubled or fearful.

JOHN 14:27 CSB

PROMISES *from* GOD'S HEART FOR *comfort…*

Blessed are those who mourn,
for they shall be comforted.

Matthew 5:4 ESV

The LORD is close to the brokenhearted;
He rescues those whose spirits are crushed.

Psalm 34:18 NLT

*Even though I walk through the
darkest valley, I will fear no evil,
for You are with me; Your rod
and Your staff, they comfort me.*

PSALM 23:4 NIV

*Blessed be the God and Father
of our Lord Jesus Christ, the
Father of mercies and the God
of all comfort. He comforts us in
all our affliction, so that we may
be able to comfort those who are
in any kind of affliction, through
the comfort we ourselves receive
from God. For just as the
sufferings of Christ overflow to
us, so also through Christ our
comfort overflows.*

II CORINTHIANS 1:3–5 CSB

The LORD gives His people strength; the LORD
blesses His people with peace.

Psalm 29:11 CSB

Because of the LORD's gracious love we are not consumed, since His compassions never end. They are new every morning.

Lamentations 3:22–23 ISV

Why am I discouraged? Why is my heart so sad? I will put my hope in God! I will praise Him again—my Savior and my God!

Psalm 42:5–6 NLT

He tends His flock like a shepherd: He gathers the lambs in His arms and carries them close to His heart.

ISAIAH 40:11 NIV

*God—He clothes me with
strength and makes my way
perfect. He makes my feet like
the feet of a deer and sets me
securely on the heights.*

PSALM 18:32–33 CSB

Come to me, all of you who are weary
and burdened, and I will give you rest.
Take up My yoke and learn from Me,
because I am lowly and humble in heart,
and you will find rest for your souls.
For My yoke is easy and My burden is light.

Matthew 11:28-30 CSB

PROMISES *from* GOD'S HEART
WHEN YOU ARE *confused...*

Trust in the LORD with all your heart and
lean not on your own understanding;
in all your ways submit to Him, and He
will make your paths straight.

Proverbs 3:5–6 NIV

God is not a God of
confusion but of peace.

1 Corinthians 14:33 NASB

*Now if any of you lacks wisdom,
he should ask God—who
gives to all generously and
ungrudgingly—and it will be
given to him.*

JAMES 1:5 CSB

The one who gets wisdom loves life; the one who cherishes understanding will soon prosper.

PROVERBS 19:8 NIV

Now we have this treasure in clay jars, so that this extraordinary power may be from God and not from us. We are afflicted in every way but not crushed; we are perplexed but not in despair; we are persecuted but not abandoned; we are struck down but not destroyed.

II Corinthians 4:7–9 CSB

The LORD leads with unfailing love and faithfulness all who keep His covenant and obey His demands.

Psalm 25:10 NLT

Obey the laws of God and follow all
His ways; keep each of His commands written
in the law of Moses so that you will prosper in
everything you do, wherever you turn.

I Kings 2:3 TLB

Now this is our boast:
Our conscience testifies that
we have conducted ourselves
in the world, and especially in
our relations with you, with
integrity and godly sincerity.
We have done so, relying not
on worldly wisdom but
on God's grace.

II CORINTHIANS 1:12 NIV

✦

PROMISES *from* GOD'S HEART
FOR *courage*…

✦

Immediately Jesus spoke to them.
"Have courage! It is I. Don't be afraid."

Matthew 14:27 CSB

I repeat, be strong and brave! Don't be afraid
and don't panic, for I, the LORD your God,
am with you in all you do.

Joshua 1:9 NET

*But Christ, God's faithful Son,
is in complete charge of God's
house. And we Christians are
God's house—He lives in us!—
if we keep up our courage firm
to the end, and our joy and
our trust in the Lord.*

HEBREWS 3:6 TLB

I have told you all this so that
you may have peace in Me.
Here on earth you will have
many trials and sorrows.
But take heart, because I have
overcome the world.

JOHN 16:33 NLT

Wait on the LORD; be of good courage,
and He shall strengthen your heart;
wait, I say, on the LORD!

Psalm 27:14 NKJV

For I am the LORD your God who takes
hold of your right hand and says to you,
do not fear; I will help you.

Isaiah 41:13 NIV

You have clothed me with strength for battle;
You subdue my adversaries beneath me.

Psalm 18:39 CSB

In Him we have boldness and confident
access through faith in Him.

Ephesians 3:12 CSB

This High Priest of ours
understands our weaknesses,
for He faced all of the same
testings we do, yet He did not
sin. So let us come boldly to the
throne of our gracious God.
There we will receive His mercy,
and we will find grace to help us
when we need it most.

HEBREWS 4:15–16 NLT

PROMISES *from* GOD'S HEART
WHEN YOU ARE *depressed…*

Why are you in despair, O my soul?
Why have you become restless and disquieted
within me? Hope in God and wait expectantly
for Him, for I shall yet praise Him, the help of
my countenance and my God.

Psalm 42:11 AMP

If your heart is broken, you'll find GOD
right there; if you're kicked in the gut,
He'll help you catch your breath.

Psalm 34:18 THE MESSAGE

He heals the brokenhearted and
binds up their wounds.

PSALM 147:3 ESV

*The Spirit of the Lord GOD
. . . has sent Me to heal the
brokenhearted . . . to comfort all
who mourn, to provide for those
who mourn in Zion; to give
them a crown of beauty instead
of ashes, festive oil instead of
mourning, and splendid clothes
instead of despair. And they will
be called righteous trees, planted
by the LORD to glorify Him.*

ISAIAH 61:1–3 CSB

I took my troubles to the LORD; I cried out to
Him, and He answered my prayer.

Psalm 120:1 NLT

Always be full of joy in the Lord;
I say it again, rejoice!
. . . Remember that the Lord
is coming soon. Don't worry
about anything; instead, pray
about everything; tell God your
needs. . . . If you do this, you will
experience God's peace. . . . His
peace will keep your thoughts
and your hearts quiet and at rest
as you trust in Christ Jesus.

PHILIPPIANS 4:4–7 TLB

Sing to LORD, you His faithful ones,
and praise His holy name. For His anger
lasts only a moment, but His favor,
a lifetime. Weeping may stay overnight,
but there is joy in the morning.

Psalm 30:4–5 CSB

PROMISES *from* GOD'S HEART
WHEN YOU ARE *discouraged*...

Have I not commanded you?
Be strong and courageous. Do not be afraid;
do not be discouraged, for the LORD your God
will be with you wherever you go.

Joshua 1:9 NIV

God blesses those who
patiently endure testing and
temptation. Afterward they
will receive the crown of life that
God has promised to those
who love Him.

JAMES 1:12 NLT

You will succeed if you
carefully follow the statutes
and ordinances the LORD
commanded Moses for Israel.
Be strong and courageous.
Don't be afraid or discouraged.

I CHRONICLES 22:13 CSB

Why, my soul, are you downcast? Why so
disturbed within me?
Put your hope in God, for I
will yet praise Him, my Savior
and my God.

Psalm 42:11 NIV

Take My yoke upon you and learn from Me,
for I am gentle and lowly in heart, and you
will find rest for your souls.

Matthew 11:29 NKJV

But as for you, be strong and don't get discouraged, for your work will be rewarded.

II Chronicles 15:7 NET

I have said these things to you,
that in me you may have peace.
In the world you will have tribulation.
But take heart; I have overcome the world.

John 16:33 ESV

I can do all this through Him
who gives me strength.

Philippians 4:13 NIV

*The LORD is the One who will
go before you. He will be with
you; He will not leave you or
abandon you. Do not be afraid
or discouraged.*

DEUTERONOMY 31:8 CSB

PROMISES *from* GOD'S HEART
WHEN YOU HAVE *doubt*...

✦ ✛

But when [Peter] saw the strength of the
wind, he was afraid, and beginning to sink he
cried out, "Lord, save me!" Immediately Jesus
reached out His hand, caught hold of him,
and said to him, "You of little faith, why did
you doubt?" When they got into the boat, the
wind ceased.

Matthew 14:30–32 CSB

Truly, I say to you, whoever
says to this mountain, "Be taken
up and thrown into the sea,"
and does not doubt in his heart,
but believes that what he says
will come to pass, it will
be done for him.

MARK 11:23 ESV

If you want to know what God wants you to do, ask Him, and He will gladly tell you, for He is always ready to give a bountiful supply of wisdom to all who ask Him; He will not resent it. But when you ask Him, be sure that you really expect Him to tell you, for a doubtful mind will be as unsettled as a wave of the sea that is driven and tossed by the wind; and every decision you then make will be uncertain, as you turn first this way and then that. If you don't ask with faith, don't expect the Lord to give you any solid answer.

JAMES 1:5–8 TLB

Jesus told them, "I tell you the truth, if you have faith and don't doubt, you can do things like this and much more. You can even say to this mountain, 'May you be lifted up and thrown into the sea,' and it will happen. You can pray for anything, and if you have faith, you will receive it."

Matthew 21:21–22 NLT

He commanded us to preach to the people and to testify that He is the one whom God appointed as judge of the living and the dead. All the prophets testify about Him that everyone who believes in Him receives forgiveness of sins through His name.

ACTS 10:42–43 NIV

PROMISES *from* GOD'S HEART
FOR *encouragement*…

✦

Do not fear, for I am with you; do not be
afraid, for I am your God. I will strengthen you;
I will help you; I will hold on to you with My
righteous right hand.

Isaiah 41:10 CSB

*God, hear my cry; pay attention
to my prayer. I call to You from
the ends of the earth when my
heart is without strength.
Lead me to a rock that is high
above me, for You have been a
refuge for me, a strong tower in
the face of the enemy.*

PSALM 61:1–3 CSB

I am sure that neither death nor
life, nor angels nor rulers,
nor things present nor things to
come, nor powers, nor height
nor depth, nor anything else in
all creation, will be able to
separate us from the love of God
in Christ Jesus our Lord.

ROMANS 8:38–39 ESV

There is no one like the God of
Jeshurun, who rides across the heavens to
help you and on the clouds in His majesty.
The eternal God is your refuge, and
underneath are the everlasting arms.

Deuteronomy 33:26–27 NIV

All praise to God, the Father of our Lord Jesus Christ. God is our merciful Father and the source of all comfort. He comforts us in all our troubles so that we can comfort others. When they are troubled, we will be able to give them the same comfort God has given us.

II Corinthians 1:3–4 NLT

This is what the LORD says, He who made the earth, the LORD who formed it and established it—the LORD is His name: "Call to me and I will answer you and tell you great and unsearchable things you do not know."

JEREMIAH 33:2–3 NIV

PROMISES *from* GOD'S HEART
FOR *endurance*…

✦

I call to God; GOD will help me. At dusk,
dawn, and noon I sigh deep sighs—He hears,
He rescues. My life is well and whole, secure.

Psalm 55:16–17 THE MESSAGE

Let us not get tired of doing good, for we will
reap at the proper time if we don't give up.

Galatians 6:9 CSB

*The LORD is my rock and my
place of safety. He is the God
who saves me. My God is my
rock. I go to Him for safety. He
is like a shield to me. He's the
power that saves me. He's my
place of safety.*

PSALM 18:2 NIRV

He gives power to the faint,
and to him who has no might he
increases strength.

ISAIAH 40:29 ESV

And not only that, but we also rejoice
in our afflictions, because we know that
affliction produces endurance, endurance
produces proven character, and proven
character produces hope. This hope will not
disappoint us, because God's love has been
poured out in our hearts through the
Holy Spirit who was given to us.

Romans 5:3–5 CSB

We continually ask God to fill you with the knowledge of His will through all the wisdom and understanding that the Spirit gives, so that you may live a life worthy of the Lord and please Him in every way: bearing fruit in every good work, growing in the knowledge of God, being strengthened with all power according to His glorious might so that you may have great endurance and patience, and giving joyful thanks to the Father, who has qualified you to share in the inheritance of His holy people in the kingdom of light.

Colossians 1:9–12 NIV

Splendor and majesty are before Him; strength and joy are in His dwelling place.

1 CHRONICLES 16:27 NIV

PROMISES *from* GOD'S HEART
FOR *eternal life...*

✦ ✛

For God loved the world in this way:
He gave His one and only Son, so that
everyone who believes in Him will not perish
but have eternal life.

John 3:16 CSB

He was pierced for our transgressions,
He was crushed for our iniquities; the
punishment that brought us peace was on
Him, and by His wounds we are healed.

Isaiah 53:5 NIV

*I tell you the truth, whoever
hears what I say and believes
in the One who sent Me has
eternal life. That person will not
be judged guilty but has already
left death and entered life.*

JOHN 5:24 NCV

For we know that if our earthly
tent we live in is destroyed, we
have a building from God, an
eternal dwelling in the heavens,
not made with hands.

II CORINTHIANS 5:1 CSB

Because You will not abandon me to the realm
of the dead, nor will you let Your faithful one
see decay. You make known to me the path of
life; You will fill me with joy in Your presence,
with eternal pleasures at Your right hand.

Psalm 16:10–11 NIV

How great are His miracles, and how
mighty His wonders! His kingdom is an
eternal kingdom, and His dominion is
from generation to generation.

Daniel 4:3 CSB

God has made everything beautiful
for its own time. He has planted eternity
in the human heart, but even so, people
cannot see the whole scope of God's
work from beginning to end.

Ecclesiastes 3:11 NLT

This is the testimony:
God has given us eternal life,
and this life is in His Son. The
one who has the Son has life.

1 JOHN 5:11–12 CSB

PROMISES *from* GOD'S HEART
FOR HIS *favor…*

✦ ✛

For You, LORD, bless the righteous one;
You surround him with favor like a shield.

Psalm 5:12 CSB

How blessed is God! And what a
blessing He is! He's the Father of our Master,
Jesus Christ, and takes us to the high places
of blessing in Him. Long before He laid down
earth's foundations, He had us in mind, had
settled on us as the focus of His love, to be
made whole and holy by His love.

Ephesians 1:5–6 THE MESSAGE

*What credit is it if you sin and are
mistreated and endure it? But
if you do good and suffer and so
endure, this finds favor with God.*

1 PETER 2:20 NET

Sing the praises of the LORD, you
His faithful people; praise His holy
name. For His anger lasts only
a moment, but His favor lasts a
lifetime; weeping may stay for the
night, but rejoicing comes in the
morning.

PSALM 30:4–5 NIV

My hand made all these things, and so they
all came into being. This is the LORD'S
declaration. I will look favorably on this kind
of person: one who is humble, submissive in
spirit, and trembles at My word.

Isaiah 66:2 CSB

Suddenly a great company of the
heavenly host appeared with the angel,
praising God and saying, "Glory to God
in the highest heaven, and on earth peace to
those on whom His favor rests."

Luke 2:13–14 NIV

Blessings on all who reverence
and trust the Lord—on all who
obey Him! Their reward shall be
prosperity and happiness. . . .
That is God's reward to those who
reverence and trust Him.

PSALM 128:1–2, 4 TLB

PROMISES *from* GOD'S HEART
WHEN YOU ARE *faithful*...

Blessings on you if I return and find you faithfully doing your work. I will put such faithful ones in charge of everything I own!

Matthew 24:46–47 TLB

The loving-kindness of the Lord is from everlasting to everlasting to those who reverence Him; His salvation is to children's children of those who are faithful to His covenant and remember to obey Him!

Psalm 103:17–18 TLB

Lying lips are detestable to the Lord, *but faithful people are His delight.*

PROVERBS 12:22 CSB

I am grateful to the One who has strengthened me, Christ Jesus our Lord, because He considered me faithful in putting me into ministry.

I TIMOTHY 1:12 NET

His master said to him, "Well done, good and faithful servant. You have been faithful and trustworthy over a little, I will put you in charge of many things; share in the joy of your master."

Matthew 25:23 AMP

Unfailing love and faithfulness protect the King; His throne is made secure through love.

Proverbs 20:28 NLT

In every situation take up the shield
of faith with which you can extinguish all
the flaming arrows of the evil one.

Ephesians 6:16 CSB

Know therefore that the LORD your
God is God; He is the faithful God,
keeping His covenant of love to a thousand
generations of those who love Him
and keep His commandments.

Deuteronomy 7:9 NIV

*Know that the LORD has
set apart the faithful for Himself;
the LORD will hear when
I call to Him.*

PSALM 4:3 CSB

✦ ✛

PROMISES *from* GOD'S HEART REGARDING *forgiveness…*

✦

In Him we have redemption,
the forgiveness of sins.

Colossians 1:14 CSB

*If you, G*OD*, kept records on
wrongdoings, who would stand
a chance? As it turns out,
forgiveness is Your habit, and
that's why You're worshiped. I
pray to G*OD*—my life a prayer—
and wait for what He'll say and
do. My life's on the line before
God, my Lord, waiting and
watching till morning.*

PSALM 130:3–6 *THE MESSAGE*

Then He took a cup, and after giving thanks, He gave it to them and said, "Drink from it, all of you. For this is My blood of the covenant, which is poured out for many for the forgiveness of sins.

MATTHEW 26:27–28 CSB

Do not judge, and you will not be judged. Do not condemn, and you will not be condemned. Forgive, and you will be forgiven.

Luke 6:37 CSB

Blessed and happy and favored are those whose lawless acts have been forgiven, and whose sins have been covered up and completely buried.

Romans 4:7 AMP

Anyone you forgive, I do too. For what
I have forgiven—if I have forgiven anything—
it is for your benefit in the presence of Christ,
so that we may not be taken advantage of by
Satan. For we are not ignorant of his schemes.

II Corinthians 2:10–11 CSB

*He is so rich in kindness and
grace that He purchased our
freedom with the blood of His
Son and forgave our sins. He
has showered His kindness on
us, along with all wisdom and
understanding.*

EPHESIANS 1:7–8 NLT

PROMISES *from* GOD'S HEART
FOR HIS *friendship*…

Friendship with God is reserved for those
who reverence Him. With them alone
He shares the secrets of His promises.

Psalm 25:14 TLB

*He guarantees right up to the
end that you will be counted
free from all sin and guilt on
that day when He returns. God
will surely do this for you, for
He always does just what He
says, and He is the one who
invited you into this wonderful
friendship with His Son,
even Christ our Lord.*

I CORINTHIANS 1:8–9 TLB

When I think of You as I lie on
my bed, I meditate on You
during the night watches
because You are my helper; I will
rejoice in the shadow of Your
wings. I follow close to You; Your
right hand holds on to me.

PSALM 63:6–8 CSB

One day Jesus was teaching . . . .
Some men came carrying a paralyzed man
on a mat. . . . When Jesus saw their faith,
He said, "Friend, your sins are forgiven."

Luke 5:17-18, 20 NIV

You make known to me the path of life;
You will fill me with joy in Your presence,
with eternal pleasures at Your right hand.

Psalm 16:11 NIV

David said this about Him:
"I keep the Lord before me always. Because
He is close by my side, I will not be hurt."

Acts 2:25 NCV

How happy is the one You choose
and bring near to live in Your
courts! We will be satisfied with
the goodness of Your house, the
holiness of Your temple.

PSALM 65:4 CSB

PROMISES *from* GOD'S HEART
FOR YOUR *future*...

"For I know the plans I have for you,"
declares the LORD, "plans to prosper
you and not to harm you, plans to give
you hope and a future."

Jeremiah 29:11 NIV

LORD, you are my portion and my cup of
blessing; You hold my future. The boundary
lines have fallen for me in pleasant places;
indeed, I have a beautiful inheritance.

Psalm 16:5–6 CSB

*Don't be envious of sinful people;
let reverence for the LORD be
the concern of your life. If it is,
you have a bright future.*

PROVERBS 23:17–18 GNT

"Do not weep any longer, for I will reward you," says the Lord. *"Your children will come back to you from the distant land of the enemy. There is hope for your future," says the* Lord.

JEREMIAH 31:16–17 NLT

Honey whets the appetite and so does wisdom! When you enjoy becoming wise, there is hope for you! A bright future lies ahead!

Proverbs 24:14 TLB

Come now, you who say, "Today or tomorrow we will travel to such and such a city and spend a year there and do business and make a profit." Yet you do not know what tomorrow will bring—what your life will be! For you are like vapor that appears for a little while, then vanishes. Instead, you should say, "If the Lord wills, we will live and do this or that."

James 4:13–15 CSB

Ask me, and I will make
the nations your inheritance,
the ends of the earth
your possession.

PSALM 2:8 NIV

✦

PROMISES *from* GOD'S HEART
WHEN YOU *give…*

✦ ✦

Give, and it will be given to you;
a good measure—pressed down, shaken
together, and running over—will be poured
into your lap. For with the measure you use,
it will be measured back to you.

Luke 6:38 CSB

*Anyone who gives one
of My most humble followers a
cup of cool water, just because
that person is My follower, will
surely be rewarded.*

MATTHEW 10:42 CEV

When you give to someone in need, don't do as the hypocrites do—blowing trumpets in the synagogues and streets to call attention to their acts of charity! I tell you the truth, they have received all the reward they will ever get. But when you give to someone in need, don't let your left hand know what your right hand is doing. Give your gifts in private, and your Father, who sees everything, will reward you.

MATTHEW 6:2–4 NLT

A poor widow came and put in two small copper coins, which make a penny. And he called his disciples to him and said to them, "Truly, I say to you, this poor widow has put in more than all those who are contributing to the offering box. For they all contributed out of their abundance, but she out of her poverty has put in everything she had, all she had to live on."

MARK 12:42–44 ESV

"Bring the whole tithe into the storehouse, that there may be food in my house. Test me in this," says the LORD Almighty, "and see if I will not throw open the floodgates of heaven and pour out so much blessing that there will not be room enough to store it."

Malachi 3:10 NIV

But remember this—if you
give little, you will get little.
A farmer who plants just a few
seeds will get only a small crop,
but if he plants much, he will
reap much. Everyone must
make up his own mind as to
how much he should give. Don't
force anyone to give more than
he really wants to, for cheerful
givers are the ones God prizes.

II CORINTHIANS 9:6–7 TLB

PROMISES *from* GOD'S HEART FOR HIS *grace*...

God saved you by His grace when you
believed. And you can't take credit for this;
it is a gift from God. Salvation is not a reward
for the good things we have done,
so none of us can boast about it.

Ephesians 2:8–9 NLT

The LORD God is a sun and shield;
The LORD bestows grace and favor and
honor; no good thing will He withhold
from those who walk uprightly.

Psalm 84:11 AMP

*The LORD laughs at those who
laugh at Him, but He gives grace
to those who are not proud.*

PROVERBS 3:34 NCV

The Word became flesh and
dwelt among us, and we have
seen His glory, glory as of the
only Son from the Father, full of
grace and truth.

JOHN 1:14 ESV

For you are saved by grace through faith,
and this is not from yourselves; it is God's gift.

Ephesians 2:8 CSB

God resists the proud, but gives
grace to the humble.

James 4:6 CSB

Each time He said, "My grace is all you need. My power works best in weakness." So now I am glad to boast about my weaknesses, so that the power of Christ can work through me.

II Corinthians 12:9 NLT

Now I [Luke] commit you to God and to the word of His grace, which can build you up and give you an inheritance among all those who are sanctified.

ACTS 20:32 NIV

✦

PROMISES *from* GOD'S HEART
WHEN YOU ARE *grieving*...

The LORD is close to the brokenhearted, and He saves those whose spirits have been crushed.

Psalm 34:18 NCV

What a wonderful God we have—He is the Father of our Lord Jesus Christ, the source of every mercy, and the One who so wonderfully comforts and strengthens us in our hardships and trials. And why does He do this? So that when others are troubled, needing our sympathy and encouragement, we can pass on to them this same help and comfort God has given us.

II CORINTHIANS 1:4 TLB

*Deep calls to deep in the roar
of Your waterfalls; all Your
breakers and Your billows have
swept over me. The LORD will
send His faithful love by day;
His song will be with me in the
night—a prayer to the
God of my life.*

PSALM 42:7–8 CSB

I will send you the Comforter—
the Holy Spirit, the source of all truth.
He will come to you from the Father
and will tell you all about Me.

John 15:26 TLB

Because of the LORD'S great love we are not
consumed, for His compassions never fail.

Lamentations 3:22 NIV

May our Lord Jesus Christ Himself and God our Father, who loved us and by His grace gave us eternal comfort and a wonderful hope, comfort you and strengthen you in every good thing you do and say.

II Thessalonians 2:16–17 NLT

Look, God's dwelling is with humanity, and He will live with them. They will be His peoples, and God Himself will be with them and will be their God. He will wipe away every tear from their eyes. Death will be no more; grief, crying, and pain will be no more, because the previous things have passed away.

REVELATION 21:3–4 CSB

PROMISES *from* GOD'S HEART FOR HIS *guidance…*

When the Spirit of truth comes,
He will guide you into all the truth.
For He will not speak on
His own, but He will speak whatever
He hears. He will also declare to
you what is to come.

John 16:13 CSB

Trust in the LORD *with all your
heart, and lean not on your own
understanding; in all your ways
acknowledge Him, and He shall
direct your paths.*

PROVERBS 3:5–6 NKJV

I will lead the blind along an unfamiliar way; I will guide them down paths they have never traveled. I will turn the darkness in front of them into light, and level out the rough ground. This is what I will do for them. I will not abandon them.

Isaiah 42:16 NET

Be strong and courageous, for you will distribute the land I swore to their ancestors to give them as an inheritance. Above all, be strong and very courageous to observe carefully the whole instruction My servant Moses commanded you. Do not turn from it to the right or the left, so that you will have success wherever you go.

JOSHUA 1:6–7 CSB

*Oh, the joys of those who do
not follow the advice of the wicked,
or stand around with sinners, or
join in with mockers. But they
delight in the law of the LORD,
meditating on it day and night.*

PSALM 1:1–2 NLT

Do not conform to the pattern of this world, but
be transformed by the renewing of your mind.
Then you will be able to test and approve what
God's will is—His good, pleasing and perfect will.

Romans 12:2 NIV

Be careful to do as the LORD your
God has commanded you; you are not to
turn aside to the right or the left. Follow the
whole instruction the LORD your God has
commanded you, so that you may live, prosper,
and have a long life in the land you will possess.

Deuteronomy 5:32–33 CSB

PROMISES *from* GOD'S HEART FOR *healing*...

He heals the brokenhearted and
bandages their wounds.

Psalm 147:3 CSB

Do not be wise in your own eyes;
fear the LORD and turn away from evil.
It will be healing to your body and
refreshment to your bones.

Proverbs 3:7–8 NASB

*Those who hope in the LORD will
renew their strength. They will
soar on wings like eagles; they will
run and not grow weary, they will
walk and not be faint.*

ISAIAH 40:31 NIV

He was pierced for our
transgressions; he was crushed
for our iniquities; upon him was
the chastisement that brought
us peace, and with his
wounds we are healed.

ISAIAH 53:5 ESV

My roots will have access to water, and the
dew will rest on my branches all night.
My whole being will be refreshed within me,
and my bow will be renewed in my hand.

Job 29:19–20 CSB

If My people who are called by My name will
humble themselves and pray and seek My face
and turn from their wicked ways, I will hear from
heaven and will forgive their sins and restore
their land. My eyes will be open and My ears
attentive to every prayer made in this place.

II Chronicles 7:14–15 NLT

Therefore we do not give up. Even though our outer person is being destroyed, our inner person is being renewed day by day.

II Corinthians 4:16 CSB

*In Your unfailing love
You will lead the people
You have redeemed. In Your
strength You will guide them
to Your holy dwelling.*

EXODUS 15:13 NIV

PROMISES *from* GOD'S HEART
FOR THE *hope of heaven...*

✦

We know that when this earthly tent we
live in is taken down (that is, when we die and
leave this earthly body), we will have a house
in heaven, an eternal body made for us by God
Himself and not by human hands.

II Corinthians 5:1 NLT

*Praise be to the God and Father
of our Lord Jesus Christ! In His
great mercy He has given us new
birth into a living hope through
the resurrection of Jesus Christ
from the dead, and into an
inheritance that can never perish,
spoil or fade. This inheritance is
kept in heaven for you.*

I PETER 1:3–4 NIV

For God loved the world in
this way: He gave His one and only
Son, so that everyone who believes
in Him will not perish
but have eternal life.

JOHN 3:16 CSB

Anyone who obeys God's laws
and teaches them will be called great
in the Kingdom of Heaven.

Matthew 5:19 NLT

I am the living bread that came down
from heaven. If anyone eats of this bread
he will live forever. The bread that I will give
for the life of the world is My flesh.

John 6:51 CSB

(It is only by God's grace that you have been saved!) For He raised us from the dead along with Christ and seated us with Him in the heavenly realms because we are united with Christ Jesus.

Ephesians 2:5–6 NLT

Our citizenship is in heaven, and we eagerly wait for a Savior from there, the Lord Jesus Christ. He will transform the body of our humble condition into the likeness of His glorious body, by the power that enables Him to subject everything to Himself.

PHILIPPIANS 3:20–21 CSB

PROMISES *from* GOD'S HEART FOR *His return…*

✦ ✦

I tell you, in the future you will see the
Son of Man seated at the right hand of Power
and coming on the clouds of heaven.

Matthew 26:64 CSB

*Now concerning how and
when all this will happen, dear
brothers and sisters, we don't
really need to write you. For you
know quite well that the
day of the Lord's return will
come unexpectedly, like a
thief in the night.*

I THESSALONIANS 5:1–2 NLT

Be patient, then, brothers and
sisters, until the Lord's coming.
See how the farmer waits for the
land to yield its valuable crop,
patiently waiting for the autumn
and spring rains.

JAMES 5:7 NIV

The Son of Man is going to come with His angels
in the glory of His Father, and then He will reward
each according to what he has done.

Matthew 16:27 CSB

The Lord Himself will come down from heaven,
with a loud command, with the voice of the
archangel and with the trumpet call of God, and
the dead in Christ will rise first. After that, we
who are still alive and are left will be caught up
together with them in the clouds to meet the Lord
in the air. And so we will be with the Lord forever.

1 Thessalonians 4:16–17 NIV

See! He is arriving, surrounded
by clouds; and every eye shall see
him—yes, and those who pierced
him. And the nations will weep
in sorrow and in terror when he
comes. Yes! Amen! Let it be so!

REVELATION 1:7 TLB

PROMISES *from* GOD'S HEART
FOR *the Holy Spirit…*

✦

I will ask the Father, and He will give you
another Counselor to be with you forever.
He is the Spirit of truth. The world is unable
to receive Him because it doesn't see Him or
know Him. But you do know Him, because He
remains with you and will be in you.

John 14:16–18 CSB

John answered them all,
"I baptize you with water,
but one who is more powerful
than I am is coming. I am not
worthy to untie the strap of His
sandals. He will baptize you with
the Holy Spirit and fire."

LUKE 3:16 CSB

Turn to me and receive
my gentle correction;
Watch and I will pour out my
spirit on you; I will share with
you my wise words in order
to redirect your lives.

PROVERBS 1:23 VOICE

I will give you a new heart and put a new spirit
within you; I will remove your heart of stone
and give you a heart of flesh. I will place My
Spirit within you and cause you to follow My
statutes and carefully observe My ordinances.

Ezekiel 36:26–27 CSB

Also, the Spirit helps us with our weakness. We do not know how to pray as we should. But the Spirit Himself speaks to God for us, even begs God for us with deep feelings that words cannot explain. God can see what is in people's hearts. And He knows what is in the mind of the Spirit, because the Spirit speaks to God for His people in the way God wants.

Romans 8:26–27 NCV

Whoever speaks a word against the Son of Man, it will be forgiven him; but whoever speaks against the Holy Spirit, it will not be forgiven him, either in this age or in the one to come.

MATTHEW 12:32 CSB

The one who keeps His commands remains in Him, and He in him. And the way we know that He remains in us is from the Spirit He has given us.

1 John 3:24 CSB

I baptize you with water for repentance, but the one who is coming after me is more powerful than I. I am not worthy to remove His sandals. He Himself will baptize you with the Holy Spirit and fire.

MATTHEW 3:11 CSB

PROMISES *from* GOD'S HEART
WHEN YOU NEED *hope*…

✦

Love the LORD, all His faithful ones.
The LORD protects the loyal, but fully
repays the arrogant. Be strong, and let
your heart be courageous, all you who
put your hope in the LORD.

Psalm 31:23–24 CSB

*Don't envy sinners, but always
continue to fear the LORD. You
will be rewarded for this; your
hope will not be disappointed.*

PROVERBS 23:17–18 NLT

*A person's steps are established
by the LORD, and He takes
pleasure in his way. Though
he falls, he will not be
overwhelmed, because the LORD
supports him with His hand.*

PSALM 37:23–24 CSB

"For I know the plans I have for you,"
declares the LORD, "plans to prosper
you and not to harm you, plans to give
you hope and a future."

Jeremiah 29:11 NIV

Through the LORD's mercies we are not
consumed, because His compassions fail not.
They are new every morning; great is Your
faithfulness. "The LORD is my portion," says
my soul, "therefore I hope in Him!"

Lamentations 3:22–24 NKJV

Therefore, since we have been justified by faith, we have peace with God through our Lord Jesus Christ. We have also obtained access through Him by faith into this grace in which we stand, and we boast in the hope of the glory of God.

Romans 5:1–2 CSB

But now he has reconciled you by Christ's physical body through death to present you holy in His sight, without blemish and free from accusation—if you continue in your faith, established and firm, and do not move from the hope held out in the gospel.

COLOSSIANS 1:22–23 NIV

PROMISES *from* GOD'S HEART
WHEN YOU NEED *humility*...

✦

How can you say to your brother, "Brother,
let me take out the speck that is in your eye," when
you yourself do not see the log that is in your own
eye? You hypocrite, first take the log out of your
own eye, and then you will see clearly to take out
the speck that is in your brother's eye.

Luke 6:42 ESV

Humility, the fear of the LORD,
results in wealth, honor, and life.

Proverbs 22:4 CSB

*Therefore, as God's chosen
people, holy and dearly loved,
clothe yourselves with
compassion, kindness, humility,
gentleness and patience.*

COLOSSIANS 3:12 NIV

*Pride leads to disgrace, but with
humility comes wisdom.*

PROVERBS 11:2 NLT

He has told you, O man, what is good;
and what does the LORD require of you but
to do justice, and to love kindness,
and to walk humbly with your God?

Micah 6:8 ESV

If my people, who are called by My name,
will humble themselves and pray and seek
My face and turn from their wicked ways,
then I will hear from heaven, and I will
forgive their sin and will heal their land.

II Chronicles 7:14 NIV

By the grace given to me I say to every
one of you not to think more highly of
yourself than you ought to think, but to think
with sober discernment, as God has distributed
to each of you a measure of faith.

Romans 12:3 NET

Whoever exalts himself will be humbled, and
whoever humbles himself will be exalted.

Matthew 23:12 ESV

*Good and upright is the LORD;
therefore He instructs sinners in His
ways. He guides the humble in what
is right and teaches them His way.
All the ways of the LORD are loving
and faithful toward those who keep
the demands of His covenant.*

PSALM 25:8–10 NIV

✦ ✦

PROMISES *from* GOD'S HEART
WHEN YOU NEED *instruction*...

I will praise the LORD who
counsels me—even at night when my
thoughts trouble me. . . . Because He is
at my right hand, I will not be shaken.

Psalm 16:7–8 CSB

Let the wise also hear and gain instruction,
and let the discerning acquire guidance!

Proverbs 1:5 NET

Whatever was written in
the past was written for our
instruction, so that we may
have hope through endurance
and through the encouragement
from the Scriptures.

ROMANS 15:4 CSB

The instruction of the LORD
is perfect, renewing one's
life; the testimony of the
LORD is trustworthy, making
the inexperienced wise. The
precepts of the LORD are
right, making the heart glad;
the command of the LORD is
radiant, making the eyes light
up. The fear of the LORD is
pure, enduring forever; the
ordinances of the LORD are
reliable and altogether righteous.
. . . In addition, Your servant is
warned by them; and in keeping
them there is abundant reward.

PSALM 19:7–9, 11 CSB

Take My yoke upon you and learn from Me, for I am gentle and humble in heart, and you will find rest for your souls.

Matthew 11:29 NIV

I have lived with integrity before Him; I've kept myself from wrongdoing. And so the LORD *restored me for my righteousness.*

PSALM 18:23–24 CEB

PROMISES *from* GOD'S HEART
FOR HIS *joy*...

✦

You will show me the path of life; in Your
presence is fullness of joy; in Your right hand
there are pleasures forevermore.

Psalm 16:11 AMP

*What happiness for those whose
guilt has been forgiven! What
joys when sins are covered over!
What relief for those who have
confessed their sins and God has
cleared their record.*

PSALM 32:2 TLB

If you keep My commands
you will remain in My love,
just as I have kept My Father's
commands and remain in
His love. I have told you
these things so that My joy
may be in you and your
joy may be complete.

JOHN 15:10–11 CSB

His glorious power will make you patient
and strong enough to endure anything,
and you will be truly happy.

Colossians 1:11 CEV

You love Him even though you have
never seen Him; though not seeing Him,
you trust Him; and even now you are happy
with the inexpressible joy that comes from
heaven itself. And your further reward for
trusting Him will be the salvation of your souls.

1 Peter 1:8–9 TLB

You have turned my mourning
into joyful dancing; You have taken
away my clothes of mourning and
clothed me with joy, that I might
sing praises to You and not be
silent. O Lord my God, I will give
You thanks forever!

PSALM 30:11–12 NLT

Now may the God of hope fill you
with all joy and peace as you believe
so that you may overflow with hope by
the power of the Holy Spirit.

Romans 15:13 CSB

✦ ✦

PROMISES *from* GOD'S HEART
FOR *justice…*

Your throne is founded on two
strong pillars—the one is Justice and
the other Righteousness. Mercy and Truth
walk before You as Your attendants.

Psalm 89:14 TLB

Then the Lord said, . . . "Will not God grant
justice to His elect who cry out to Him day and
night? Will He delay helping them? I tell you
that He will swiftly grant them justice."

Luke 18:6–8 CSB

*The Lord does what is right,
and He loves justice. So honest
people will see His face.*

PSALM 11:7 ICB

True justice must be given to foreigners living among you and to orphans, and you must never accept a widow's garment as security for her debt.

DEUTERONOMY 24:17 NLT

Here is My servant, whom I uphold,
My chosen One in whom I delight;
I will put My Spirit on Him, and He
will bring justice to the nations.

Isaiah 42:1 NIV

The LORD sits enthroned forever;
He has established His throne for judgment.
And He judges the world with righteousness;
He executes judgment on the nations with
fairness. The LORD is a refuge for the
persecuted, a refuge in times of trouble.

Psalm 9:7–9 CSB

The God of Israel has spoken;
the protector of Israel said to
me: "The king who rules with
justice, who rules in obedience
to God, is like the sun shining
on a cloudless dawn, the sun
that makes the grass
sparkle after rain."

II SAMUEL 23:3–4 GNT

✦ ✦

PROMISES *from* GOD'S HEART
WHEN YOU ARE *lonely*...

Draw near to God,
and He will draw near to you.

James 4:8 CSB

*The LORD is my shepherd; I have
all that I need. He lets me rest
in green meadows; He leads
me beside peaceful streams. He
renews my strength. He guides
me along right paths, bringing
honor to His name. Even when I
walk through the darkest valley, I
will not be afraid, for You are close
beside me. Your rod and Your staff
protect and comfort me.*

PSALM 23:1–4 NLT

Call on Me and come and pray to
Me, and I will listen to you. You
will seek Me and find Me when
you seek Me with all
your heart.

JEREMIAH 29:12–13 NIV

For I am persuaded that neither
death nor life, nor angels nor rulers, nor things
present nor things to come, nor powers, nor
height nor depth, nor any other created thing
will be able to separate us from the love of
God that is in Christ Jesus our Lord!

Romans 8:38–39 CSB

He has said: "I will never leave
you nor forsake you."

Hebrews 13:5 ESV

Praise be to the God and Father of our Lord Jesus Christ. God is the Father who is full of mercy and all comfort. He comforts us every time we have trouble, so when others have trouble, we can comfort them with the same comfort God gives us.

II Corinthians 1:3–4 NCV

The Lord is fair in everything He does and full of kindness. He is close to all who call on Him sincerely. He fulfills the desires of those who reverence and trust Him; He hears their cries for help and rescues them.

PSALM 145:17–19 TLB

PROMISES *from* GOD'S HEART
FOR HIS STEADFAST *love*...

All the paths of the LORD lead to gracious love and truth for those who keep His covenant and His decrees.

Psalm 25:10 ISV

"Though the mountains move and the hills shake, My love will not be removed from you and My covenant of peace will not be shaken," says your compassionate LORD.

Isaiah 54:10 CSB

For God so loved the world that He gave His one and only Son, that whoever believes in Him shall not perish but have eternal life.

JOHN 3:16 NIV

The person who has My
commandments and obeys them
is the one who loves Me. The one
who loves Me will be loved by My
Father, and I will love him and will
reveal myself to him.

JOHN 14:21 NET

When the kindness and the love of
God our Savior toward man appeared,
not by works of righteousness which we
have done, but according to His mercy He saved
us, through the washing of regeneration and
renewing of the Holy Spirit.

Titus 3:4–5 NKJV

May our Lord Jesus Christ Himself
and God our Father, who has loved
us and given us eternal encouragement
and good hope by grace, encourage your
hearts and strengthen you in every
good work and word.

2 Thessalonians 2:16–17 CSB

*L*ORD, *Your love reaches*
to the heavens, Your loyalty
to the skies.

PSALM 36:5 NCV

PROMISES *from* GOD'S HEART
FOR HIS *mercy*…

The Lord is very
compassionate and merciful.

James 5:11 NKJV

But as for me, I will sing each
morning about Your power and
mercy. For You have been my
high tower of refuge, a place of
safety in the day of my distress.

PSALM 59:16 TLB

We do not have a high priest
incapable of sympathizing with
our weaknesses, but One who
has been tempted in every way
just as we are, yet without sin.
Therefore let us confidently
approach the throne of grace
to receive mercy and find grace
whenever we need help.

HEBREWS 4:15–16 NET

What a contrast between Adam and
Christ who was yet to come! And what a
difference between man's sin and God's
forgiveness! For this one man, Adam, brought
death to many through his sin. But this one
man, Jesus Christ, brought forgiveness to
many through God's mercy.

Romans 5:14–15 TLB

Praise be to the LORD, for He has heard my cry for mercy. The LORD is my strength and my shield; my heart trusts in Him, and He helps me.

Psalm 28:6–7 NIV

He who conceals his transgressions will not prosper, But whoever confesses and turns away from his sins will find compassion and mercy.

PROVERBS 28:13 AMP

PROMISES *from* GOD'S HEART FOR WHEN YOU ARE WORRIED ABOUT *money*…

✦

Wealth gained quickly will dwindle away,
but the one who gathers it little by
little will become rich.

Proverbs 13:11 NET

Honor the LORD *with your
wealth and with the best part
of everything you produce.
Then He will fill your barns with
grain, and your vats will
overflow with good wine.*

PROVERBS 3:9–10 NLT

Whenever you give to the poor, don't sound a trumpet before you, as the hypocrites do in the synagogues and on the streets, to be applauded by people. Truly I tell you, they have their reward. But when you give to the poor, don't let your left hand know what your right hand is doing, so that your giving may be in secret. And your Father who sees in secret will reward you.

MATTHEW 6:2–4 CSB

Evil men borrow, but do not repay their debt, but the godly show compassion and are generous.

Psalm 37:21 NET

Why do you spend money for what
is not bread, and your wages for what
does not satisfy? Listen carefully to Me, and
eat what is good, and let your soul delight
itself in abundance. Incline your ear, and
come to Me. Hear, and your soul shall live;
and I will make an everlasting covenant with
you—the sure mercies of David.

Isaiah 55:2–3 NKJV

*Keep your life free from the
love of money. Be satisfied with
what you have, for He Himself
has said, I will never leave you
or abandon you.*

HEBREWS 13:5 CSB

PROMISES *from* GOD'S HEART
WHEN YOU ARE *obedient*…

Those who teach God's laws and obey them
shall be great in the Kingdom of Heaven.

Matthew 5:19 TLB

The LORD *gives wisdom; from*
His mouth come knowledge and
understanding. He stores up
success for the upright; He is a
shield for those who live with
integrity so that He may guard
the paths of justice and protect
the way of His faithful followers.

PROVERBS 2:6–8 CSB

"If you follow My decrees and are careful to obey My commands, I will send you the seasonal rains. The land will then yield its crops, and the trees of the field will produce their fruit."

LEVITICUS 26:3–4 NLT

If only you had obeyed My commandments, prosperity would have flowed to you like a river, deliverance would have come to you like the waves of the sea.

Isaiah 48:18 NET

The one who keeps His commands remains in Him, and He in him. And the way we know that He remains in us is from the Spirit He has given us.

1 John 3:24 CSB

Obey me, and I will be your God and you
shall be My people; only do as I say,
and all shall be well!

Jeremiah 7:23 TLB

Though your sins are scarlet,
they will be as white as snow; though
they are crimson red, they will be like wool.
If you are willing and obedient, you will
eat the good things of the land.

Isaiah 1:18–19 CSB

*Surely, LORD, You bless the
righteous; You surround them
with Your favor as with a shield.*

PSALM 5:12 NIV

✦ ✦

PROMISES *from* GOD'S HEART
WHEN YOU ARE FEELING *overwhelmed…*

A person's steps are established
by the LORD, and He takes pleasure in his
way. Though he falls, he will not be
overwhelmed, because the LORD
supports him with His hand.

Psalm 37:23–24 CSB

*You who answer prayer, to
You all people will come. When we
were overwhelmed by sins, You
forgave our transgressions. Blessed
are those You choose and bring near
to live in Your courts!*

PSALM 65:2–4 NIV

Come to Me, all of you
who are weary and burdened, and I
will give you rest.

MATTHEW 11:28 CSB

God is our refuge and strength,
always ready to help in times of trouble.

Psalm 46:1 NLT

The God of all grace, who has called you to his
eternal glory in Christ, will himself restore, confirm,
strengthen, and establish you.

1 Peter 5:10 ESV

You, LORD, are a shield around me, my glory,
and the One who lifts up my head.

Psalm 3:3 CSB

*Cast your burden on
the* LORD—*He will support you!
God will never let the
righteous be shaken!*

PSALM 55:22 CEB

PROMISES *from* GOD'S HEART
WHEN YOU NEED *peace*...

The LORD gives His people strength;
the LORD blesses His people with peace.

Psalm 29:11 CSB

*Don't worry about anything;
instead, pray about everything;
tell God your needs, and don't
forget to thank Him for His
answers. If you do this, you will
experience God's peace, which
is far more wonderful than the
human mind can understand. His
peace will keep your thoughts and
your hearts quiet and at rest as
you trust in Christ Jesus.*

PHILIPPIANS 4:6–7 TLB

Let the peace that comes
from Christ rule in your hearts.
For as members of one body you
are called to live in peace.
And always be thankful.

COLOSSIANS 3:15 NLT

But the fruit of the Spirit is love, joy, peace,
patience, kindness, goodness, faithfulness,
gentleness, and self-control.

Galatians 5:22 CEB

Abundant peace belongs to those
who love Your instruction; nothing
makes them stumble.

Psalm 119:165 CSB

Peace I leave with you. My peace I give you.
I give to you not as the world gives.
Don't be troubled or afraid.

John 14:27 CEB

*Fill my heart with joy when
their grain and new wine abound.
In peace I will lie down and sleep,
for You alone, Lord, make me
dwell in safety.*

PSALM 4:7–8 NIV

PROMISES *from* GOD'S HEART
FOR HIS *power...*

You will receive power when the
Holy Spirit has come on you.

Acts 1:8 CSB

Tell everyone about God's power. His majesty
shines down on Israel; His strength is mighty in
the heavens. God is awesome in His sanctuary.
The God of Israel gives power and strength to
His people. Praise be to God!

Psalm 68:34–35 NLT

*Fan into flame the gift of God,
which is in you through the
laying on of my hands. For the
Spirit God gave us does not
make us timid, but gives us
power, love and self-discipline.*

II TIMOTHY 1:6–7 NIV

Jesus has the power of God.
His power has given us
everything we need to live
and to serve God. We have
these things because we know
Him. Jesus called us by His
glory and goodness.

II PETER 1:3 ICB

Now I know that the LORD saves His anointed
one; God answers His anointed one from His
heavenly sanctuary, answering with mighty acts
of salvation achieved by His strong hand.

Psalm 20:6 CEB

He gives strength to the faint and
strengthens the powerless.

Isaiah 40:29 CSB

The kingdom of God does
not consist in talk but in power.

1 Corinthians 4:20 ESV

*For who is God, except the
LORD? And who is a rock,
except our God? It is God who
arms me with strength, and
makes my way perfect. He makes
my feet like the feet of deer, and
sets me on my high places.*

PSALM 18:31–33 NKJV

✦ ✦

PROMISES *from* GOD'S HEART FOR WHEN YOU *praise Him…*

LORD, You are my God; I will exalt You.
I will praise Your name, for You have
accomplished wonders, plans formed
long ago, with perfect faithfulness.

Isaiah 25:1 CSB

Praise the LORD, my soul;
all my inmost being,
praise His holy name.

PSALM 103:1 NIV

I will give thanks to the LORD with all my
heart; I will tell of all Your wonders.

Psalm 9:1 NASB

Then I heard every creature
in heaven and on earth and
under the earth and on the sea,
and all that is in them, saying:
"To him who sits on the throne
and to the Lamb be praise and
honor and glory and power,
for ever and ever!"

REVELATION 5:13 NIV

PROMISES *from* GOD'S HEART
WHEN YOU *pray*…

Call to Me and I will answer you
and tell you great and incomprehensible
things you do not know.

Jeremiah 33:3 CSB

When you pray, go into your
most private room, close the
door and pray to your Father
who is in secret, and your Father
who sees [what is done] in
secret will reward you.

MATTHEW 6:6 AMP

How the king rejoices in your strength, O LORD! He shouts with joy because You give him victory. For You have given him his heart's desire; You have withheld nothing he requested. You welcomed him back with success and prosperity. You placed a crown of finest gold on his head.

PSALM 21:1–3 NLT

Confess your sins to each other and pray for each other so that you may be healed. The prayer of a righteous person is powerful and effective.

James 5:16 NIV

Keep on asking, and you will
receive what you ask for. Keep on
seeking, and you will find. Keep on
knocking, and the door will be opened
to you. For everyone who asks, receives.
Everyone who seeks, finds. And to everyone
who knocks, the door will be opened.

Matthew 7:7–8 NLT

*Now if any of you lacks
wisdom, he should ask God—
who gives to all generously
and ungrudgingly—and it
will be given to him.*

JAMES 1:5 CSB

Depart from me, all you who
do iniquity, for the LORD has
heard the voice of my weeping.
The LORD has heard my
supplication, the LORD receives
my prayer. All my enemies
will be ashamed and greatly
dismayed; they shall
turn back, they will
suddenly be ashamed.

PSALM 6:8–10 NASB

PROMISES *from* GOD'S HEART
FOR HIS *presence* IN YOUR LIFE...

The LORD is in His holy temple;
the LORD—His throne is in heaven.
His eyes watch; His gaze examines everyone.

Psalm 11:4 CSB

You lead me in the path of life.
I experience absolute joy in
Your presence; You always
give me sheer delight.

PSALM 16:11 NET

From one man He made all the nations, that they should inhabit the whole earth; and He marked out their appointed times in history and the boundaries of their lands. God did this so that they would seek Him and perhaps reach out for Him and find Him, though He is not far from any one of us.

ACTS 17:26–27 NIV

Let all who take refuge in You rejoice;
let them shout for joy forever. . . .
For You, LORD, bless the righteous one;
You surround him with favor like a shield.

Psalm 5:11–12 CSB

Neither death nor life, neither angels nor demons, neither the present nor the future, nor any powers, neither height nor depth, nor anything else in all creation, will be able to separate us from the love of God that is in Christ Jesus our Lord.

Romans 8:38–39 NIV

[The LORD] replied,
"My presence will go with you,
and I will give you rest."

EXODUS 33:14 CSB

His glory is great in Your
salvation; honor and majesty
You have placed upon him.
For You have made him most
blessed forever; You have made
him exceedingly glad with Your
presence. For the king trusts
in the LORD, and through the
mercy of the Most High he
shall not be moved.

PSALM 21:5–7 NKJV

PROMISES *from* GOD'S HEART
FOR HIS *provision…*

✦

Young lions lack food and go hungry,
but those who seek the LORD will
not lack any good thing.

Psalm 34:10 CSB

*Bring the full tithe into the
storehouse, that there may be
food in my house. And thereby
put me to the test, says the LORD
of hosts, if I will not open the
windows of heaven for you and
pour down for you a blessing
until there is no more need.*

MALACHI 3:10 ESV

From the sky You send rain
on the hills, and the earth is
filled with Your blessings. You
make grass grow for the cattle
and plants for us to use, so that
we can grow our crops . . . and
bread to give us strength.

PSALM 104:13–15 GNT

The Spirit of the Lord GOD is upon me . . .
to bring good news to the poor; he has
sent me to bind up the brokenhearted, to
proclaim liberty to the captives, and the
opening of the prison to those who are
bound . . . to give them a beautiful headdress
instead of ashes, the oil of gladness instead
of mourning, the garment of praise instead of
a faint spirit; that they may be called oaks of
righteousness, the planting of the LORD,
that he may be glorified.

Isaiah 61:1, 3 ESV

And my God will meet all your
needs according to the riches of
His glory in Christ Jesus.

Philippians 4:19 NIV

*Consider the ravens: They don't
sow or reap; they don't have a
storeroom or a barn; yet God
feeds them. Aren't you worth
much more than the birds?*

LUKE 12:24 CSB

PROMISES *from* GOD'S HEART
FOR YOUR *protection*…

You are being guarded by God's power
through faith for a salvation that is ready
to be revealed in the last time.

1 Peter 1:5 CSB

God will command His angels to
protect you wherever you go.

Psalm 91:11 CEV

*The fear of man brings a
snare, but one who trusts in
the* LORD *will be protected.*

PROVERBS 29:25 NASB

*Hide Your loved ones in the
shelter of Your presence, safe
beneath Your hand, safe from all
conspiring men. Blessed is the
Lord, for He has shown me that
His never-failing love protects me
like the walls of a fort!*

PSALM 31:20–21 TLB

He will cover you with His feathers;
you will take refuge under His wings.
His faithfulness will be a protective shield.

Psalm 91:4 CSB

Now to Him who is able to protect you from
stumbling, and to make you stand in the
presence of His glory, blameless with great joy,
to the only God our Savior, through Jesus Christ
our Lord, be glory, majesty, dominion, and
authority before all time and now and forever.

Jude 24 NASB

The LORD loves justice,
and He will never abandon the godly.
He will keep them safe forever.

Psalm 37:28 NLT

*A man is a fool to trust
himself! But those who use
God's wisdom are safe.*

PROVERBS 28:26 TLB

PROMISES *from* GOD'S HEART
FOR HIS *purpose* FOR YOU...

"For I know the plans I have for you," declares the
LORD, "plans to prosper you and not to harm you,
plans to give you hope and a future."

Jeremiah 29:11 NIV

And we know that all things work together for good
for those who love God, who are called according
to His purpose, because those whom He foreknew
He also predestined to be conformed to the image
of His Son, that His Son would be the firstborn
among many brothers and sisters.

Romans 8:28–29 NET

*"Follow Me," He told
them, "and I will make
you fish for people!"*

MATTHEW 4:19 CSB

God has given us this task of
reconciling people to Him.
For God was in Christ, reconciling
the world to Himself, no longer
counting people's sins against them.
And He gave us this wonderful
message of reconciliation.

II CORINTHIANS 5:18–19 NLT

He said to him, "You shall love the
Lord your God with all your heart and with
all your soul and with all your mind. This is the
great and first commandment. And a second is
like it: You shall love your neighbor as yourself.
On these two commandments depend all
the Law and the Prophets."

Matthew 22:37–40 ESV

You yourselves, as living stones,
a spiritual house, are being built to be a holy
priesthood to offer spiritual sacrifices acceptable
to God through Jesus Christ.

1 Peter 2:5 CSB

I am single-minded: Forgetting
the things that are behind and
reaching out for the things that
are ahead, with this goal in mind,
I strive toward the prize of the
upward call of God in Christ
Jesus. . . . But our citizenship is
in heaven—and we also eagerly
await a savior from there, the
Lord Jesus Christ, who will
transform these humble bodies
of ours into the likeness of His
glorious body by means of that
power by which He is able to
subject all things to Himself.

PHILIPPIANS 3:13–14, 20–21 NET

PROMISES *from* GOD'S HEART
FOR *rest and renewal…*

✦

Those who trust in the LORD will
renew their strength; they will soar on
wings like eagles; they will run and not become
weary; they will walk and not faint.

Isaiah 40:31 CSB

[The Lord] lets me rest in the meadow
grass and leads me beside the quiet streams.
He gives me new strength. He helps me do
what honors Him the most.

Psalm 23:2–3 TLB

*Come to Me, all of you who are
weary and carry heavy burdens,
and I will give you rest.*

MATTHEW 11:28 NLT

*That's why we are not discouraged.
No, even if outwardly we are
wearing out, inwardly we are being
renewed each and every day.*

II CORINTHIANS 4:16 ISV

The law of the LORD is perfect,
restoring the soul; the testimony of the
LORD is sure, making wise the simple.

Psalm 19:7 NASB

Take off your former way of life, the old self that
is corrupted by deceitful desires, to be renewed
in the spirit of your minds; and . . . put on the new
self, the one created according to God's likeness
in righteousness and purity of the truth.

Ephesians 4:22–24 CSB

Take my yoke upon you, and learn
from me, for I am gentle and lowly in heart,
and you will find rest for your souls.

Matthew 11:29 ESV

[He] redeems your life from
destruction, [He] crowns you with
loveingkindness and tender mercies,
[He] satisfies your mouth with good things,
so that your youth is renewed like the eagle's.

Psalm 103:4–6 NKJV

*Do not be conformed to this
world, but be transformed by
the renewal of your mind, that
by testing you may discern what
is the will of God, what is good
and acceptable and perfect.*

ROMANS 12:2 ESV

PROMISES *from* GOD'S HEART
FOR *self-control*…

✦ ✛

Everyone who competes exercises
self-control in everything. However,
they do it to receive a perishable crown,
but we an imperishable crown.

I Corinthians 9:25 CSB

*For freedom Christ has
set us free. Stand firm, then,
and do not be subject again to
the yoke of slavery.*

GALATIANS 5:1 NET

By His divine power, God has given us everything we need for living a godly life. We have received all of this by coming to know Him, the One who called us to Himself by means of His marvelous glory and excellence. . . . In view of all this, make every effort to respond to God's promises. Supplement your faith with a generous provision of moral excellence, and moral excellence with knowledge, and knowledge with self-control, and self-control with patient endurance, and patient endurance with godliness, and godliness with brotherly affection, and brotherly affection with love for everyone. The more you grow like this, the more productive and useful you will be in your knowledge of our Lord Jesus Christ.

II PETER 1:3, 5–8 NLT

LORD, who can dwell in Your tent? Who can live on
Your holy mountain? The one who
lives blamelessly, practices righteousness,
and acknowledges the truth in his heart.

Psalm 15:1–2 CSB

God didn't give us a spirit that is timid but one that
is powerful, loving, and self-controlled.

II Timothy 1:7 CEB

*The LORD is good and
upright; therefore He instructs
sinners in the way. . . . All the paths
of the LORD are faithfulness and
truth to those who comply with His
covenant and His testimonies. For
the sake of Your name, LORD, forgive
my wrongdoing, for it is great.*

PSALM 25:8, 10–11 NASB

PROMISES *from* GOD'S HEART
FOR *spiritual gifts…*

God also testified by signs and wonders, various miracles, and distributions of gifts from the Holy Spirit according to His will.

Hebrews 2:4 CSB

But the Holy Spirit produces this kind of fruit in our lives: love, joy, peace, patience, kindness, goodness, faithfulness, gentleness, and self-control. There is no law against these things!

Galatians 5:22–23 NLT

You also, like living stones, are being built into a spiritual house to be a holy priesthood, offering spiritual sacrifices acceptable to God through Jesus Christ.

1 PETER 2:5 NIV

Now as we have many parts in one body, and all the parts do not have the same function, in the same way we who are many are one body in Christ and individually members of one another. According to the grace given to us, we have different gifts: If prophecy, use it according to the proportion of one's faith; if service, use it in service; if teaching, in teaching; if exhorting, in exhortation; giving, with generosity; leading, with diligence; showing mercy, with cheerfulness.

ROMANS 12:4–8 CSB

Let love be your greatest aim; nevertheless, ask also for the special abilities the Holy Spirit gives, and especially the gift of prophecy, being able to preach the messages of God. But if your gift is that of being able to "speak in tongues," that is, to speak in languages you haven't learned, you will be talking to God but not to others, since they won't be able to understand you. You will be speaking by the power of the Spirit, but it will all be a secret. But one who prophesies, preaching the messages of God, is helping others grow in the Lord, encouraging and comforting them.

1 Corinthians 14:1–3 TLB

There are different kinds
of spiritual gifts, but the same
Spirit gives them. There are
different ways of serving, but
the same Lord is served. There
are different abilities to perform
service, but the same God gives
ability to all for their particular
service. The Spirit's presence is
shown in some way in each
person for the good of all.

I CORINTHIANS 12:4–7 GNT

PROMISES *from* GOD'S HEART FOR WHEN YOU *stray...*

The one who conceals his sins
will not prosper, but whoever confesses
and renounces them will find mercy.

Proverbs 28:13 CSB

*If a man has a hundred sheep, and
one wanders away and is lost,
what will he do? Won't he leave the
ninety-nine others and go out into
the hills to search for the lost one?
And if he finds it, he will rejoice
over it more than over the ninety-
nine others safe at home!*

MATTHEW 18:12–13 TLB

*Suppose a woman has ten silver
coins and loses one. Won't she light
a lamp and sweep the entire house
and search carefully until she finds
it? And when she finds it, she will
call in her friends and neighbors
and say, "Rejoice with me because
I have found my lost coin."*

LUKE 15:8–9 NLT

In Him we have redemption,
the forgiveness of sins.

Colossians 1:14 CSB

Go and learn what this means: "I desire mercy
and not sacrifice." For I did not come to call the
righteous, but sinners, to repentance."

Matthew 9:13 NKJV

His father said to the servants,
"Quick! Bring the finest robe in the
house and put it on him. Get a ring for
his finger and sandals for his feet. And kill
the calf we have been fattening. We must
celebrate with a feast, for this son of mine was
dead and has now returned to life. He was lost,
but now he is found." So the party began.

Luke 15:22–24 NLT

If you return, I will take you back;
you will stand in My presence.

Jeremiah 15:19 CSB

The Son of Man has come to save
that which was lost.

MATTHEW 18:11 NKJV

PROMISES *from* GOD'S HEART
WHEN YOU NEED *strength*...

He gives power to the weak and
strength to the powerless.

Isaiah 40:29 NLT

The LORD is the strength of His people; He is a
stronghold of salvation for His anointed.

Psalm 28:8 CSB

*Behold, the Lord GOD will
come with might, with His arm
ruling for Him. Behold, His
compensation is with Him, and
His reward before Him.*

ISAIAH 40:10 NASB

He makes both us and you
remain strong in the faith
because we belong to Christ.
He anointed us.

II CORINTHIANS 1:21 NIRV

Those who hope in the LORD will
renew their strength. They will soar on
wings like eagles; they will run and not grow
weary; they will walk and not be faint.

Isaiah 40:31 NIV

I pray that the eyes of your heart will
have enough light to see what is the hope
of God's call, what is the richness of God's
glorious inheritance among believers, and
what is the overwhelming greatness of God's
power that is working among us believers.
This power is conferred by the energy of
God's powerful strength.

Ephesians 1:18–19 CEB

All those who come and listen and obey Me are like a man who builds a house on a strong foundation laid upon the underlying rock. When the floodwaters rise and break against the house, it stands firm, for it is strongly built.

LUKE 6:47–48 TLB

PROMISES *from* GOD'S HEART WHEN YOU *tithe...*

"Bring the whole tithe into the storehouse, that there may be food in my house. Test me in this," says the LORD Almighty, "and see if I will not throw open the floodgates of heaven and pour out so much blessing that there will not be room enough to store it."

Malachi 3:10 NIV

Give generously to them and do so without a grudging heart; then because of this the LORD your God will bless you in all your work and in everything you put your hand to.

DEUTERONOMY 15:10 NIV

Honor the LORD with your possessions, and with the firstfruits of all your increase; so your barns will be filled with plenty, and your vats will overflow with new wine.

PROVERBS 3:9–10 NKJV

Each person should do as he has decided in his heart—not reluctantly or out of compulsion, since God loves a cheerful giver. And God is able to make every grace overflow to you, so that in every way, always having everything you need, you may excel in every good work.

II Corinthians 9:7–8 CSB

All the tithe of the land, whether of the seed of the land or of the fruit of the tree, is the LORD'S. It is holy to the LORD.

Leviticus 27:30 NKJV

Bring the best of the firstfruits of your land to the house of the LORD your God.

Exodus 23:19 CSB

Give to others, and God will give to you.
Indeed, you will receive a full measure,
a generous helping, poured into your hands—
all that you can hold. The measure you use for
others is the one that God will use for you.

Luke 6:38 GNT

*Now regarding your question about
the money being collected for God's
people in Jerusalem. You should
follow the same procedure I gave to
the churches in Galatia. On the first
day of each week, you should each
put aside a portion of the money
you have earned.*

I CORINTHIANS 16:1–2 NLT

It is possible to give away
and become richer! It is also
possible to hold on too tightly
and lose everything. Yes, the
liberal man shall be rich!
By watering others,
he waters himself.

PROVERBS 11:24–25 TLB

✦ ✦

PROMISES *from* GOD'S HEART
WHEN YOU ARE FACING *trials…*

✦

Though now for a short time, if necessary,
you suffer grief in various trials so that the
proven character of your faith—more valuable
than gold which, though perishable, is refined
by fire—may result in praise, glory, and honor
at the revelation of Jesus Christ.

1 Peter 1:6–7 CSB

*Dear brothers and sisters, when
troubles of any kind come your way,
consider it an opportunity for great
joy. For you know that when your faith
is tested, your endurance has a chance
to grow. So let it grow, for when your
endurance is fully developed, you will be
perfect and complete, needing nothing.*

JAMES 1:2–4 NLT

*Fear not, for I am with you;
be not dismayed, for I am your
God; I will strengthen you, I will
help you, I will uphold you with
my righteous right hand.*

ISAIAH 41:10 ESV

God will bless you, if you don't give
up when your faith is being tested. He will
reward you with a glorious life, just as he
rewards everyone who loves Him.

James 1:12 CEV

Blessed be the Lord! Day after day He bears
our burdens; God is our salvation.

Psalm 68:19 CSB

Stoop down and reach out to those
who are oppressed. Share their burdens,
and so complete Christ's law.

Galatians 6:2 THE MESSAGE

Your promise revives me; it comforts
me in all my troubles. The proud hold me in
utter contempt, but I do not turn away from
Your instructions. I meditate on Your age-old
regulations; O LORD, they comfort me.

Psalm 119:50–52 NLT

*For our momentary light
affliction is producing for us
an absolutely incomparable
eternal weight of glory.*

II CORINTHIANS 4:17 CSB

PROMISES *from* GOD'S HEART FOR HIS *truth...*

You will know the truth,
and the truth will set you free.

John 8:32 CSB

The sum of Your word is truth, and every one
of Your righteous rules endures forever.

Psalm 119:160 ESV

*This is what the LORD says—
your Redeemer, the Holy One
of Israel: "I am the LORD your
God, who teaches you what is
best for you, who directs you in
the way you should go."*

ISAIAH 48:17 NIV

I have hidden your word in my heart that I might not sin against you. Praise be to you, LORD.

PSALM 119:11–12 NIV

God! His way is perfect; the LORD's word is tried and true. He is a shield for all who take refuge in Him.

Psalm 18:30 CEB

Therefore everyone who hears these words of Mine and puts them into practice is like a wise man who built his house on the rock. The rain came down, the streams rose, and the winds blew and beat against that house; yet it did not fall, because it had its foundation on the rock.

Matthew 7:24–25 NIV

Truthful lips will be established forever, but a lying tongue is [credited] only for a moment.

Proverbs 12:19 AMP

In Him you also were sealed with the promised Holy Spirit when you heard the word of truth, the gospel of your salvation, and when you believed. The Holy Spirit is the down payment of our inheritance, until the redemption of the possession, to the praise of His glory.

Ephesians 1:13–14 CSB

*In the exercise of His will
He gave us birth by the word of
truth, so that we would be
a kind of first fruits among
His creatures.*

JAMES 1:18 NASB

PROMISES *from* GOD'S HEART FOR HIS *victory*...

✦ ✦

Now I know that the LORD gives victory
to His anointed; He will answer him
from His holy heaven with mighty
victories from His right hand.

Psalm 20:6 CSB

I put no trust in my bow, my sword does not
bring me victory; but You give us victory
over our enemies, You put our adversaries to
shame. In God we make our boast all day long,
and we will praise Your name forever.

Psalm 44:6–8 NIV

*The horse is prepared for the
day of battle, but victory
belongs to the LORD.*

PROVERBS 21:31 NLT

*The sting of death is sin,
and the power of sin is the law.
But thanks be to God! He
gives us the victory through
our Lord Jesus Christ.*

I CORINTHIANS 15:56–57 NIV

Everyone who has been born of God
conquers the world. This is the victory
that has conquered the world: our faith.

I John 5:4 CSB

The righteous will never be moved; he will be
remembered forever. He is not afraid of bad
news; his heart is firm, trusting in the LORD.
His heart is steady; he will not be afraid, until
he looks in triumph on his adversaries.

Psalm 112:6–8 ESV

The LORD is on my side; I will not fear.
What can man do to me? The LORD is on
my side as my helper; I shall look in
triumph on those who hate me.

Psalm 118:6–7 ESV

We have been made right with
God because of our faith. So we
have peace with God through
our Lord Jesus Christ. Through
our faith, Christ has brought us
into that blessing of God's grace
that we now enjoy. And we are
happy because of the hope we
have of sharing God's glory.

ROMANS 5:1–2 ICB

PROMISES *from* GOD'S HEART
WHEN YOU ARE *weak and weary*...

✦ +

"Come to Me, all you who are weary and
burdened, and I will give you rest.
Take My yoke upon you and learn from
Me, for I am gentle and humble in heart,
and you will find rest for your souls."

Matthew 11:28–29 NIV

*Remember Your word to
Your servant; You have given
me hope through it. This is my
comfort in my affliction: Your
promise has given me life.*

PSALM 119:49–50 CSB

I always let the LORD guide me.
Because He is at my right hand,
I will not be shaken.
Therefore my heart is glad and
my whole being rejoices;
my body also rests securely.

PSALM 16:8–9 CSB

"My grace is all you need. My power
works best in weakness." So now I am glad to
boast about my weaknesses, so that the power
of Christ can work through me.

II Corinthians 12:9 NLT

For the moment all discipline seems painful rather than pleasant, but later it yields the peaceful fruit of righteousness to those who have been trained by it. Therefore lift your drooping hands and strengthen your weak knees, and make straight paths for your feet, so that what is lame may not be put out of joint but rather be healed.

Hebrews 12:11–13 ESV

So let's not get tired of doing what is good. At just the right time we will reap a harvest of blessing if we don't give up.

Galatians 6:9 NLT

As for you, brethren, do not grow weary in doing good.

II THESSALONIANS 3:13 NKJV

PROMISES *from* GOD'S HEART
WHEN YOU ARE *worried...*

Don't worry about your life, what you
will eat or what you will drink; or about
your body, what you will wear. Isn't life
more than food and the body more than
clothing? Consider the birds of the sky:
They don't sow or reap or gather into barns,
yet your heavenly Father feeds them.
Aren't you worth more than they?

Matthew 6:25–26 CSB

The LORD *is my strength
and shield. I trust Him with all
my heart. He helps me, and my
heart is filled with joy.*

PSALM 28:7 NLT

*Do not be anxious about
anything, but in everything by
prayer and supplication with
thanksgiving let your requests
be made known to God. And the
peace of God, which surpasses
all understanding, will guard
your hearts and your
minds in Christ Jesus.*

PHILIPPIANS 4:6–7 ESV

In God I trust and am not afraid.
What can man do to me?

Psalm 56:11 NIV

I will be glad and rejoice in Your love,
for You saw my affliction and knew the
anguish of my soul. You have not given
me into the hands of the enemy but
have set my feet in a spacious place.

Psalm 31:7–8 NIV

Trust in the LORD with all your heart, and do not rely on your own understanding; in all your ways know Him, and He will make your paths straight.

Proverbs 3:5–6 CSB

Don't let your heart be troubled. Believe in God; believe also in Me.

John 14:1 CSB

He will vindicate you in broad daylight, and publicly defend your just cause. Wait patiently for the Lord! Wait confidently for Him! Do not fret over the apparent success of a sinner, a man who carries out wicked schemes. Do not be angry and frustrated. Do not fret. That only leads to trouble.

PSALM 37:6–8 NET

PROMISES *from* GOD'S HEART
FOR HIS *wisdom…*

✦

If any of you lacks wisdom, you should ask
God, who gives generously to all without
finding fault, and it will be given to you.

James 1:5 NIV

To obey the LORD *is*
the fundamental principle
for wise living; all who carry
out His precepts acquire
good moral insight. He will
receive praise forever.

PSALM 111:10 NET

The LORD gives wisdom; from
His mouth come knowledge and
understanding. He stores up
success for the upright; He is a
shield for those who live with
integrity so that He may guard
the paths of justice and protect
the way of His faithful followers.

PROVERBS 2:6–8 CSB

Because of God you are in Christ Jesus, who
has become for us wisdom from God. In Christ
we are put right with God, and have been
made holy, and have been set free from sin.

1 Corinthians 1:30 NCV

How wonderful to be wise, to understand
things, to be able to analyze them and
interpret them. Wisdom lights up a
man's face, softening its hardness.

Ecclesiastes 8:1 TLB

In Him we have redemption through His blood, the forgiveness of sins, in accordance with the riches of God's grace that He lavished on us. With all wisdom and understanding.

Ephesians 1:7–8 NIV

This also comes from the LORD of Armies. He gives wondrous advice; He gives great wisdom.

Isaiah 28:29 CSB

In Him lie hidden all the treasures of wisdom and knowledge.

Colossians 2:3 NLT

To the person who is pleasing in His sight, He gives wisdom, knowledge, and joy.

ECCLESIASTES 2:26 CSB

PROMISES *from* GOD'S HEART
FOR *work*...

Commit your work to the LORD,
and your plans will succeed.

Proverbs 16:3 CEB

The hardworking farmer ought to be
the first to get a share of the crops.

II Timothy 2:6 CSB

*Anyone who does not provide
for their relatives, and especially
for their own household, has
denied the faith.*

I TIMOTHY 5:8 NIV

*In all hard work there
is profit, but merely talking
about it only brings poverty.*

PROVERBS 14:23 NET

Let the favor of the Lord our God
be on us; establish for us the work of
our hands—establish the work of our hands!

Psalm 90:17 CSB

Whatever you do, work heartily,
as for the Lord and not for men.

Colossians 3:23 ESV

The LORD will send rain at the proper
time from His rich treasury in the heavens
and will bless all the work you do.

Deuteronomy 28:12 NLT

God blessed the seventh
day and made it a holy day.
He made it holy because on that
day He rested. He rested from
all the work He had done in
creating the world.

GENESIS 2:3 ICB

*I can do all things through
Christ who strengthens me.*

PHILIPPIANS 4:13 NKJV

Do all things without complaining
and disputing, that you may become
blameless and harmless, children of God
without fault in the midst of a crooked and
perverse generation, among whom you
shine as lights in the world.

Philippians 2:14-15 NKJV

You will enjoy the fruit of your labor.
How joyful and prosperous you will be!

Psalm 128:2 NLT